THE STORY OF WATER
A MOVING ADVENTURE

Diane Bair

Contents

Rigby
A Harcourt Achieve Imprint

www.Rigby.com
1-800-531-5015

A World of Water

You've been playing in the yard all day, and now it's time for a bath! You fill up the bathtub, maybe add some soap bubbles, and then scrub yourself clean. When your bubbly bath water starts to cool off, you run a little more warm water, and … ah, it sure feels good. But where did that water come from? Did you know that you might be bathing in the same water the dinosaurs drank over 200 million years ago?

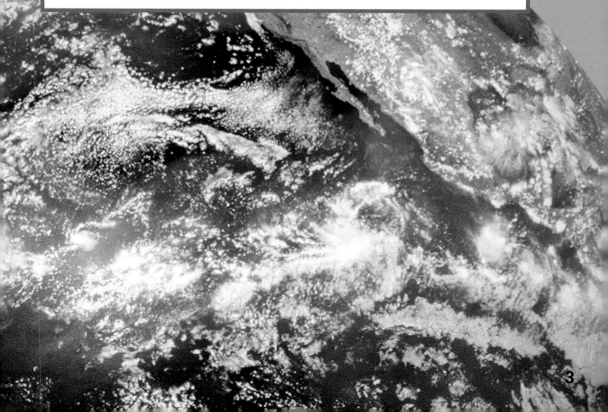

Before you say "Yuck!" think about this—water is on a never-ending journey between Earth and the sky. We have all of the water that we will ever have. In fact, you might call water the most recycled thing on the planet.

First let's look at the big, and very wet, picture. Water may be one of the most important things on Earth because where there is no water, there is no life. When you see pictures taken of Earth from far away, our planet looks blue because it is almost completely covered with water.

In fact, water covers nearly 75 percent of the world. The water found in lakes, puddles, the ocean, and in clouds is all joined together. Water is moving all the time. We call this moving water the "water cycle."

How do trees and plants fit into this water cycle? And why do we need water in the first place? Do we have enough water? Come along as we answer these and many more questions in *The Story of Water!*

Why do we need water?

Every plant and animal needs water to live. Human beings are watery creatures with water making up over 60 percent of our bodies. That means we can't survive without water for more than a few days.

There's a water cycle happening inside our bodies, too. Water flows through our blood and moves oxygen to our cells. Water helps remove wastes from our bodies through urine and sweat, and it helps keep our body temperature where it should be, while also protecting our joints and organs.

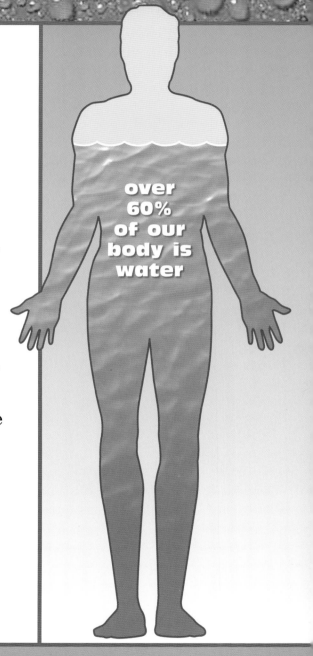

over 60% of our body is water

Did you know that every part of the human body is made of water? Bones are made up of 22 percent water, the brain is over 75 percent water, muscles are 75 percent water, blood is 83 percent water, and the liver is made up of 96 percent water. If we didn't drink water every day, our bodies would not work the way they should.

We lose water when we perspire, or sweat, and when we use the bathroom. We also lose water by **exhalation**, or breathing out, because there is even water in our breath!

Our bodies also get the water we need when we drink such things as fruit juice and milk, and by eating fruits and vegetables. Soft drinks and colas don't count because they actually cause water loss.

How much do we need to drink to make up for the water we lose every day? Doctors say that eight to ten cups of water is about right for most people. However, if you play sports, you sweat more, so you need more water. When you get sick, you lose water from your body as well, so you need to drink as much as you can. Did you know that people feel better when their bodies have enough water? So the next time you feel worn out or too tired to do your homework, drink a glass of water and see if it helps!

What happens to a raindrop?

That depends on where the raindrop falls. If a raindrop lands in a body of water, it might just go with the flow. If it hits the ground, it might run into a nearby body of water or a storm drain. It might also soak into the ground and move along with the **groundwater**.

Water Surprises

Raindrops are not shaped like teardrops. Lab experiments that stopped raindrops in midair showed that raindrops are actually flat on the bottom like hamburger buns.

Take a look at this drawing to see what happens to water that soaks into the ground. The groundwater trickles down until it hits solid bedrock and cannot go anywhere else. The groundwater just sits there, making the soil deep underground very wet. The top layer of this very wet area is called the **water table**.

Near the ocean where there is a lot of groundwater, the water table is really close to the surface. In drier places, such as the desert where there is very little groundwater, the water table can be from 200 to 600 feet below the surface.

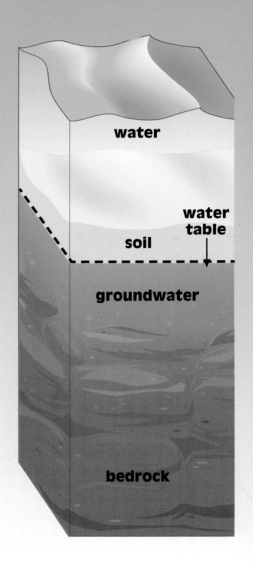

The Water Table

water

water table

soil

groundwater

bedrock

Of course, like all water, groundwater keeps moving. It flows slowly until it reaches a stream, river, lake, pond, or ocean. Groundwater might continue its underground journey until it flows out from a hillside spring or pours over rocks along the roadside. It might also be drawn out of the ground from a well. Some families get their drinking water out of wells.

How do trees and plants fit into the water cycle?

From the tiniest shoots to the largest trees, plants use their roots to pull water from the soil. Inside the plant, water travels through the trunk or stem and out to its leaves. If you take a leaf and look at the underside of it with a microscope, you'll see tiny holes. These holes send water out into the air, much like our skin allows us to sweat. In plants, this is called transpiration.

Water Wonders

A full-grown tree can give off as much as 40,000 gallons of water per year—enough to fill a very large swimming pool!

What happens to water in lakes and ponds?

It might spend a season or two changing back and forth between a liquid and a solid, freezing and melting. Water in a lake or pond might be heated by the sun, **evaporate**, and rise into the air as **water vapor**.

Once the water vapor rises, it cools and condenses, or turns from a gas into a liquid made up of tiny droplets. We see these millions and millions of water droplets as clouds.

When a cloud becomes so heavy with droplets that air currents can't hold the cloud up anymore, the water falls back to Earth as rain, which is called **precipitation**. If the air is cold enough, the water falls as snow or hail.

Then the whole cycle begins again. The water in lakes and ponds keeps evaporating and condensing as the water cycle keeps going around and around.

The Water Cycle

condensation

evaporation

precipitation

runoff

Water Trivia

The largest hailstone ever recorded in the United States was 17.5 inches around, and it weighed 1.67 pounds. That's larger than a softball! This monster ice ball fell in Coffeyville, Kansas, in September 1970.

How much does a cloud weigh?

Those white, fluffy-looking clouds appear to be as light as giant cotton balls, yet they contain enough ice and water droplets to weigh half a million tons! Huge, black thunderstorm clouds may weigh several million tons.

What are some other ways water is special?

Water is one of the only things on our planet that can be a liquid, a solid, or a gas. If water were a superhero, its special power would be shape-shifting! If you boil water, it turns to steam. If you freeze it, water changes into ice.

Water has the power to change the shape of other materials, too. Over time, water can carve solid rock into beautiful shapes and dig caves out of rock.

Do we have enough water?

Actually, we may not have enough water to last forever. Water covers most of the planet's surface, yet only a small amount of it is OK for people to drink. Over 97 percent of water is found in the oceans as saltwater. Removing salt from saltwater to make clean water we can drink is expensive.

Two percent of our water is in the form of glaciers, which are huge mountains of ice floating in the ocean, and ice caps, which sit on top of snowy mountains. That leaves just 1 percent of Earth's water to supply our daily needs.

What effect do people have on the water supply?

The more people there are on Earth, the more water we need. Every year the world's population grows, which means all of these new people also need food to eat. It takes water to grow food. Therefore, the more food we need, the more water we need to grow it. All over the world, water tables are falling because we're taking water out of the ground faster than the water cycle can refill it.

Some places are very dry because they have **droughts**. Other places get plenty of rain, yet they don't have enough water because it is too polluted, or dirty, to drink.

Where are the wettest and driest places on Earth?

The best place in the world to be an umbrella salesperson would probably be Cherrapunji in India, where 100 inches of rain once fell in four days! During the rainy season there, it can rain for two months without stopping.

Where is the driest spot on Earth? The Atacama Desert in Chile is the driest place on Earth. Parts of this desert haven't seen a drop of rain since humans started measuring rainfall amounts a very long time ago! At the center of this land is a place that scientists call "absolute desert." Even though this part of the world is terribly dry, more than one million people live in the Atacama Desert today.

What is water pollution?

As water travels on its never-ending journey between Earth and the sky, it sometimes mixes with other materials. Some of these, unfortunately, are pollutants, which are substances that are harmful to living things. When factory smokestacks blow pollutants into the air, those pollutants soon fall back to Earth with the rain and snow. When we put dangerous chemicals such as pesticides onto the land, or bury **toxic** materials underground, all we are doing is harming the environment.

These toxic materials sometimes end up in the groundwater, and that can **contaminate** the water we drink. Factories that dump their wastes into rivers and streams kill fish and make water unhealthy for people to drink. Fertilizers and chemicals flow from farmlands and into waterways, polluting them. In the water cycle, what goes around, comes around. Everything is connected.

How does water get clean again?

Strangely enough, dirt can make water cleaner! Soil is made up of rock material and tiny pieces of plants and animals. When water flows through, it helps to remove pollutants. This is called filtering water.

Nature has other ways of keeping water clean, too. Tiny, one-celled creatures called bacteria destroy pollutants in water by eating waste materials. Evaporation even helps clean up water, because when water evaporates, it leaves lots of waste matter behind. One example of this is when water evaporates off the ocean. It leaves its salt behind!

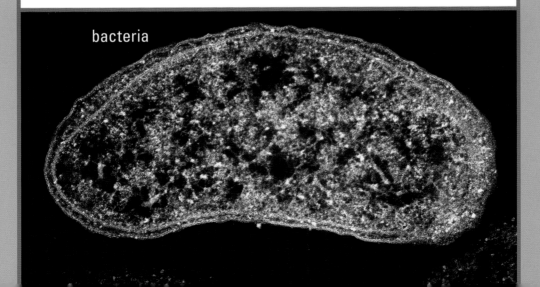

bacteria

This is Your
drinking Water
**PLEASE DO NOT
POLLUTE**
Fishing By
Permit Hoiders
Only

NORTH
WEST
WATER

⚠️
**DANGER DEEP
WATER**

NO SWIMMING

How does water get into our faucets?

Drinking water comes from groundwater, such as wells and springs, or from surface water, such as rivers, lakes, and man-made **reservoirs**. Groundwater supplies are pumped out, cleaned to make them drinkable, and then delivered to homes through pipes.

Surface water is pumped to a water treatment plant, where it passes through several cleaning stages. It is **filtered** many times to remove tiny bits of plants, dirt, grit, and poisonous chemicals. You wouldn't want to have those in your glass of water!

Then, bright UV lights are flashed onto the water to kill germs. **Disinfectants** are sometimes added to remove any germs the water might pick up as it makes its journey to homes and businesses.

Groundwater that goes into homes might only make a short trip from a family's backyard well to a pipe that goes right to their home. But surface water often makes a longer trip, going through miles and miles of underground pipes before it reaches the faucets of homes and businesses. Large underground pipes, called water mains, are hidden far beneath city streets and buried under fields in the countryside.

How Wastewater Gets Clean

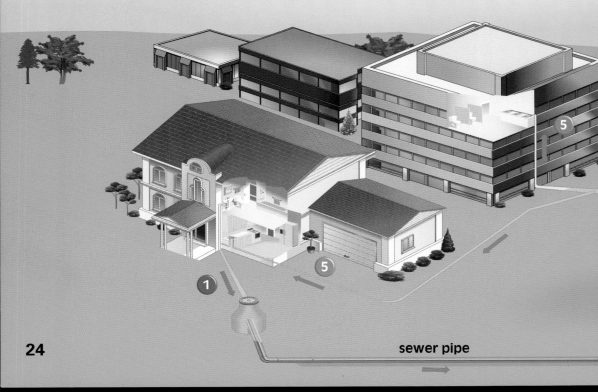

sewer pipe

Where does the dirty water go?

Clean drinking water comes into our homes through one set of pipes and leaves as **wastewater** through another set of pipes. Dirty wastewater that we flush down the toilet or that disappears down the drain must be cleaned so that it can be recycled—and, of course, used again and again!

1 Wastewater leaves the home through the sewer.

2 Water is filtered.

3 UV lights are used to kill germs.

4 Disinfectants are added.

5 Clean water is reused.

water main

water treatment plant

water pump

How much water do we use every day?

The average person in the United States uses 65 gallons of water a day for washing, drinking, and doing laundry. It sounds like a lot, but think about it. You use water every time you flush the toilet, shower, bathe, and brush your teeth. Then there are outdoor uses, such as washing the car and watering the yard. It all adds up! About 75 percent of the water we use is in the bathroom (the toilet is a major water guzzler)!

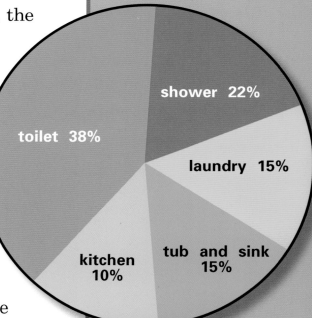

Average Household Uses of Water

- shower 22%
- toilet 38%
- laundry 15%
- kitchen 10%
- tub and sink 15%

Water **conservation** experts say we waste as much as 40 percent of the water we use. One leaky toilet can waste more than 50 gallons of water a day. A dripping faucet can waste 75 to 1,000 gallons of water per week!

One way you can help to save water is to do a little detective work. Do you have sneaky leaks at your house? Ask an adult where your water meter is (it has numbers on it that show how much water is used). Write down the numbers on the water meter. Then wait an hour, making sure that no one uses any water in your home. Check it again, and if the numbers have changed, you've got at least one leak!

Besides fixing leaks, you can save water in other ways such as repairing old toilets and using low-flow shower heads that use less water than regular shower heads.

Water-saving Tips

Unless you're a plumber, you probably can't fix leaky pipes, faucets, and toilets, but there are lots of other ways you can save water.

1. If you turn off the tap while brushing your teeth, you will save 4–10 gallons a day.
2. Never use your toilet as a wastebasket—put tissues in the trash! You can save 3–7 gallons per flush.
3. Don't take LONG showers! A short shower will get you clean, and you can save 3–7 gallons per minute.

4. If you fill the sink when you wash and rinse dishes, instead of letting the water run, you will save 8–15 gallons per day.
5. Wash outdoor items, such as bikes and trash cans, on the lawn to give your grass an extra drink.
6. When you wash the car, wet it quickly, turn off the spray, and then wash it with soapy water from a bucket. Try to rinse quickly so you don't waste any water.

Conclusion

That's the story of the water cycle. If you've come this far, you've taken a long, wet trip yourself—and you're probably thirsty, so enjoy a glass of water and think about what a journey the water's been on.

Glossary

bedrock a solid layer of rock found under soil, dirt, sand, and water

conservation to use something carefully to keep from wasting it

contaminate to make something dirty or unclean

disinfectant something that cleans, such as soap

drought a long period of time with no rain

evaporate to heat a liquid until it has changed into a gas

exhalation the act of breathing out

filter to take the dirt and unclean materials out of water by pouring it through something

groundwater water found below the Earth's surface

reservoir a natural or man-made pond or lake that is used to hold water

wastewater dirty water that has been used and is no longer needed

water table the top layer of groundwater

water vapor water that has been evaporated and is a gas

Index